NORTHAMPTON THEN & NOW

IN COLOUR

PHILIP SAWFORD

The History Press

First published in 2013

The History Press
The Mill, Brimscombe Port
Stroud, Gloucestershire, GL5 2QG
www.thehistorypress.co.uk

British Library Cataloguing in Publication Data.
A catalogue record for this book is available from the British Library.

ISBN 978 0 7524 8785 4

Typesetting and origination by The History Press
Printed in India.

CONTENTS

ACKNOWLEDGEMENTS

Special thanks are due to Rebecca Willis for her endless patience, and to my father for the extended loan of numerous source materials.

ABOUT THE AUTHOR

Philip Sawford has a degree in contemporary military and international history and a postgraduate diploma in museum studies, and has volunteered in several smaller museums local to Northamptonshire. He is currently restoring his home, a 200-year-old blacksmith's cottage in Irthliongborough, Northants. This is his first book for The History Press.

INTRODUCTION

This is a book of contrasts. Over the course of the following pages, you will see how Northampton has changed. Many of the town's well-known and well-loved buildings have now gone forever, but some street scenes, apart from the modern shop frontages, remain relatively unchanged. A few photographs, thankfully, bear a reasonably true resemblance to the originals. It is for the reader to make up their own mind on the results of the town's modernisations and improvements. What cannot be disputed, however, is just how much has changed.

During the medieval period Northampton was one of the most important towns in the country. Its importance and strategic location on the river Nene was marked by the building of a great castle. Since then, Northampton's national importance has dwindled – but the town has always been prosperous. It grew initially out of the castle's walls, and by the mid-twentieth century had absorbed most of its surrounding villages to become the largest town in Europe. The town was rebuilt after the Great Fire of 1675, with only a few original buildings surviving. What was rebuilt was in turn replaced by the prosperous Victorians – financed by the wealth of the industrialised boot and shoe trade – until pre-Victorian Northampton was only visible in the town's street plans. Many of these Victorian buildings have now gone, replaced in their turn by the Modernist architecture of the post-war years.

Due to the lack of widespread photography before the invention of dry-plate photography in 1879, the original images in this book date from around the 1880s to the 1950s. The modern photographs were taken at the end of the summer of 2012.

Where possible, the modern photographs have been taken from the same spot. However, there are some exceptions: trying to take acceptable photographs from the original vantage-point is sometimes harder than it may sound. For one, many of these old-time photographers had a particular habit of taking their photographs from the middle of a road. This sort of recklessness in many of Northampton's roads today would result in either a very blurry photograph or a very injured photographer. For these reasons, I was not always able to achieve an exact replica of the 'then' image's viewpoint. Other than the need to avoid traffic, the one thing which continuously scuppered the ability to take a modern photograph from the same location was street furniture. The culprit, more often than not, was the road signs: it is not until you look at old photographs that you realise how pervasive a problem they have become in the modern street. Not only are they often ugly, but also many of them are completely unnecessary.

The entries in this book have been arranged roughly as they would occur in a journey through Northampton from east to west. This is for no other reason than that it is the direction from which I would always travel to the town centre.

The original images have been taken from my own collection. The modern images, in order to avoid heavy traffic detracting from the images, were mainly taken in the morning.

ST JOHN'S HOSPITAL, WESTON FAVELL

ST JOHN'S HOSPITAL in 1911, now known as St John's Residential Care Home, sits on Wellingborough Road. It has stood on its current site since 1879. The previous St John's, at the bottom of Bridge Street, was closed when the site was redeveloped as a railway station. It was originally opened, on the Wellingborough Road site, as a charitable convalescent home. It is not just the name and site which have been retained: the modern-day residential care home continues in the tradition of St John's and operates as a charity. Its elderly residents are housed in forty-four modern bedrooms. It even has its own in-house laundry and hairdressing salon. In the summer, children from the neighbouring Church of England primary school visit and play games on the front lawn, much to the residents' delight. The original façade of the building has been preserved, along with many original

internal fixtures and fittings, but the rear of the building has been extended to allow for modern facilities and additional bedrooms. From the front lawn, however, many of these changes cannot be seen, and the building still retains its original Victorian charm and character. The original gatehouse has also survived.

ORIGINALLY, WESTON FAVELL was a village in its own right. It was recorded in the Domesday Book simply as 'Westone'. The Favell part was added due to a later connection with a family of the same name who took ownership of the parish. The village slowly expanded over the years until, in the 1930s, the parish's 2,000 acres actually included parts of Abington. It was eventually absorbed into Northampton in 1965, at a time when the town was rapidly expanding. In the 1970s Weston Favell became an expansion area in its own right and expanded well beyond the old village boundaries. It even had its own shopping centre and multi-storey car park by 1974. Some of the old village still remains in the middle of this vast urban area around St Peter's church, which is the oldest surviving building in Weston Favell.

ABINGTON PARK LAKES

ABINGTON PARK IS located on the site of a medieval village. This image was taken in around 1897. The village was demolished to make way for the manor house's walled deer park. This occurred during the time of the great enclosures of the seventeenth century. This particular part of Northampton was given back to the people when the park was opened to the public in 1897. In its day it was a major local attraction, with lakes, ornamental beds and tree-lined promenades. Abington Park, with 117 acres, was a place for leisure and recreation. When the park was opened, three ornamental lakes were formed from the old spring which supplied the manor house; the first and highest lake was turned into a boating lake and paddling pool. It is located next to the old water tower and pigeonry, which was built for William Thursby in 1678. The two lower lakes were ornamental.

AS THESE TWO images show, some things never change. The lakes are still as popular with families who wish to feed the ducks today as they ever were. People can even be seen fishing in the lakes, which proves how healthy the lakes have become in recent years. Although the park is not as popular a leisure venue as it once was, it is still an important local facility and has benefited from recent improvements and upgrades. In addition to the more traditional activities, members of the public can now use a range of outdoor fitness equipment. The park also hosts outdoor events such as the annual Green Festival.

THE CHURCH OF
ST PETER AND ST PAUL

THE CHURCH IS mentioned in the Domesday Book but the main body of the church only dates back to 1821, when it was rebuilt. This image shows the church in around 1920. The church would have originally been for the use of the family and staff of the manor house. The previous church on the site would have been for the lost village. It is known locally as the church in the park. The church has not had any significant alterations.

The gate and surrounding wall in this picture are still in place and in good condition. The only major difference today is that the trees in the churchyard have matured. The church is still an active place of worship, with a choir, a children's worker and an active Mother's Union. Along with the manor house, the building is one of the centrepieces of Abington Park.

VISITORS CAN ALSO find the farmhouse and farm buildings, once let out to a tenant farmer, in the grounds of the old manor house. It is known as Cockerill's Farm, and is named after a former occupant. Today it is

used as offices and a storage facility for the park's maintenance team. There is also a small office where the hire of the tennis courts can be arranged. There are rudimentary changing facilities and a public toilet. On the Wellingborough Road you will find Archway Cottages. These were once a part of the manor's estate. The Northampton Corporation did plan to demolish them in the 1930s, but a local campaign saved them from demolition. They were used as residential accommodation for many years and have recently been sold.

ABINGTON MUSEUM

ABINGTON MANOR DATES back to 1500 (this image was taken in around 1950) and was once home to Shakespeare's granddaughter Elizabeth Hall, who lived there for twenty years from 1649. The original hall was a lot smaller than it is today. It was extended in the 1660s, and additional rooms were built to surround the great hall. In 1669 the house was sold to a Mr William Thursby, who was an MP for Northampton. By 1743 the house had been extended again and remodelled in the Georgian style. It remained in the Thursby family until 1841, when the house had to be sold. After the sale, the house was used as a private mental asylum before being given to the town by Lady Wantage in 1892. The estate was opened as a public park in 1897 in celebration of Queen Victoria's Diamond Jubilee. It was opened by

Alderman H.E. Randall and, like many estates in Northamptonshire, was surrounded by high stone walls in order to keep out poachers and undesirables. These were torn down when the park was opened up to the public but some sections, reduced in height, do still remain. The majority of the stone walls were replaced by cast-iron railings. The house was not opened to the public until 1899, when it was turned into a museum.

THE MUSEUM IS still open today and retains many of its original Victorian exhibits. The Victorian idea of a museum was to enlighten the average man on the great subjects of the arts and the sciences. The museum contained many taxidermy displays, as well as fossils found in the local area. In 1994 the museum was updated and improved. Today the museum seeks mainly to interpret the local history of the surrounding area through exhibitions such as 'Northampton Life: From the cradle to the grave'. It also houses the Regimental Museum of both the Northamptonshire Regiment and the Northamptonshire Yeomanry. The building is now Grade I listed and still retains the aviary known as the Bird Walk.

ABINGTON PARK
BANDSTAND

BANDSTANDS BECAME POPULAR in Britain after the Royal Horticultural Society erected one in their South Kensington garden in 1861. By the end of the nineteenth century, any town of a reasonable size had its own bandstand. The one in Abington Park, shown here in 1909, was erected in 1900. It became a major attraction and many of the most famous bands of the day performed there. This included such bands as Her Majesty's Grenadier Guards. The bandstand was originally surrounded by an iron fence, which was probably

removed for salvage during the Second World War. Within the confines of this inner circle, spectators could, for the sum of 6*d*, rent a deckchair for the day. After years of neglect, the bandstand was restored and repainted in its original colours in 1997.

ALTHOUGH NOWHERE NEAR as popular as it used to be, the bandstand does still play host to a range of concerts and performances over the course of the summer. These concerts, combined with refreshments from the Park Café, make for an enjoyable day out. The first café to be opened in the park was called the Abington Park Refreshment Rooms. It opened in 1898 and a cup of tea and a sandwich would have cost you the reasonable sum of 3*d*; today a cup of coffee and a panini in the Park Café would cost a considerable amount more.

15

THE DRILL HALL

THE OLD DRILL hall on Clare Street, pictured here in around 1914, is one of Northampton's best-kept architectural secrets. It was built in a neo-Gothic style in 1859 at a cost of £7,000. This was during the era of the Rifle Volunteer Movement, the precursor to the modern-day Territorial Army. The hall was home to the regimental headquarters and to A Squadron of the Northamptonshire Yeomanry, which was the cavalry equivalent to the foot-slogging Rifle Volunteers. Its ranks were filled with the upper and middle classes of society, and as a result the regiment's Drill Halls were often very elaborate. Like their uniform, the Drill Hall of each unit was unique to that unit. It was used during both the First and Second World War. At the end of the Second World War it was used as a Military Dispersal Unit, more

commonly known as a demob centre. Men who had served their time with 'the Colours' were transported into Northampton by train; at the train station there was a sign simply saying, 'This way for Civvy Street'. Once the men had correctly followed the directions to the Drill Hall they were given their new documentation, final pay packet and a 'civvy suit'. The men were given a choice between a couple of styles of suit and a choice of two hats. In addition, they were also given a suitcase in which to carry their new belongings.

TODAY THE DRILL Hall is still used by the Territorial Army. It is now used by C (Leicestershire and Northamptonshire) Company, 3rd Battalion, Royal Anglian Regiment, and 118 Recovery Company, Royal Electrical and Mechanical Engineers. It is also used by the local Army Cadet Force. The castellations and chimneys seen in the photograph (left) have been subsequently removed at an unknown date. Unit markings are now displayed proudly on the building's face. These denote the various units which now share the Drill Hall.

GARDEN OF REMEMBRANCE

THE GARDEN OF Remembrance, in Abington Street, pictured here in 1938, a year after it opened. It proudly recorded the names of the men of the town who gave their lives for King and Country in the First World War; 2,906 names are displayed on a wall of remembrance. In pride of place in the centre of the garden stands a memorial to Lieutenant Colonel Edgar Roberts Mobbs DSO. Mobbs was the captain of Northampton Saints, the rugby football team, at the outbreak of the war. He also, by that time, had seven caps for England. When the First World War broke out he tried to enlist, but was told that he was too old to gain a commission. Undeterred, Mobbs went about forming his own company of 250 men. These were to become known as the 'Sportsmen' or 'Mobbs' Own'. He went on to gain a commission and Mobbs'

Company went on to form the backbone of the 7th Battalion of the Northamptonshire Regiment. Mobbs died in action at the Battle of Passchendaele in 1917. Like the true leader that he was, he died leading his men from the front. A memorial to Mobbs and the men of his battalion was erected in Market Square and unveiled by Lord Lilford in July 1921. The memorial remained in Market Square until 1937, when it moved to its current location.

THE REMEMBRANCE GARDEN has not changed much since 1937. It is still a fitting tribute to the men of the town who made the ultimate sacrifice in the First World War. It was amended after the Second World War to include the names of those lost during that conflict. It is still kept in very good order, and the council ensure that the garden is still bedecked in flowers every year. The only change to have occurred since 1937 is the addition of the ornate metal fencing which now encloses the wall of remembrance. This feature was added to protect the wall, due in part to the number of vagrants who use the covered area as a resting place.

CHARLES BRADLAUGH'S MONUMENT

THIS OLD PHOTOGRAPH of Charles Bradlaugh's monument was taken in 1910. Bradlaugh was a prominent politician, political activist and well-known atheist. He was the MP for Northampton from 1880 to 1891. He was, however, prevented from taking his seat in the House of Commons as the duly elected representative for Northampton until 1886, as he refused to take the Oath of Allegiance to the Crown, which finished with the phrase, 'so help me God'. He instead wished only to affirm his allegiance. In 1888, therefore, he secured the passage of the Oaths Act, which ensured that in future all MPs had the right to affirm their allegiance instead of taking a religious oath. Bradlaugh was also an advocate of Trade Unionism and women's suffrage. He was also responsible for setting up the National Secular Society in 1866. He was a much-loved figure, and over 3,000 people attended his funeral.

BRADLAUGH HAS NOT been totally forgotten in Northampton. Not only is his statute still standing tall in Abington Square, but also his name has been given to a local park, a hall at the University of Northampton and, most importantly, a public house. The

modern photograph shows that Bradlaugh's monument is the only feature that has survived the passage of time. The private residences in the background of the picture have gone, demolished to make way for a modern terrace of shops and a Jaguar garage. The monument has not survived the passage of time completely unscathed: the railings that once embellished and protected the monument have long since gone, most probably due to the Second World War's demand for scrap metal. In more recent times, Bradlaugh himself has been damaged: on more than one occasion, for example, his outstretched pointing finger has been snapped clean off.

ABINGTON SQUARE

ABINGTON SQUARE, WHEN it was open to two-way traffic on both Kettering Road and Wellingborough Road, *c.* 1950. Bradlaugh's monument had lost its railings by this point and had instead been surrounded by a traffic island, which was laid with a patch of grass and floral borders. The monument itself was moved forward, towards the town centre, when the Garden of Remembrance was built in 1937. The lack of traffic in the 1950s is demonstrated by the fact that two cars have actually parked next to Bradlaugh's monument.

THE MODERN IMAGE shows the one-way system that is needed to cope with the heavy flow of traffic in this area of town. What is clearly visible today is the excessive

amount of road markings which now cover the surface of most modern roads.

Joining Bradlaugh in the centre of Abington Square is now a very sizeable mast which houses a CCTV camera. This camera oversees this busy student area. At night pubs such as the Penny Whistle and the Racehorse are frequented by many of Northampton University's 14,000 students. In addition to these night-time venues, just out shot of the right-hand side of the image, can be found Urban Tiger. This 'gentleman's club' is housed in the old Abington Square Mission. What the Revd E .T. Prust, who laid the foundation stone in 1878, would have thought of the eventual use of this once religious and philanthropic building can only be imagined.

ABINGTON STREET

DOMINATING THE BACKGROUND of this 1906 image is the building which once housed the People's Café. It was run by the Blue Ribbon temperance organisation. It gave the working man another alternative to public houses for both socialisation and sustenance. After suffering a serious fire, it was repaired and turned into a leather warehouse and then a billiard hall. It was demolished in 1933 and part of the site was used for the memorial gardens.

The No. 6 tram, which is heading towards the camera and down Abington Street, was one of the original trams that had an opentop deck, which exposed the passengers to the elements. Either side of the tram are a series of ornate pillars that were used to support the tram's power cables. These were needed all along the tram routes. This image shows just how much the town's streets changed when the electrified trams were introduced. When the first motorised buses came along, from 1923 onwards, they would use the area behind Bradlaugh's monument as a makeshift bus stop. These solid-wheeled Thorneycroft buses would run routes all the way to Wellingborough and back.

APART FROM THE obvious demolition of the People's Café, the structural nature of the image has not changed significantly. The changes are starker when you contrast the shop frontages. The sun awnings and intricate shop frontages have gone, replaced by a series of cheaply produced plastic shop signs and frontages.

The Old Cock public house has been replaced by The Bantam. Just past The Bantam, you can see the new road junction which was put in place in 1989 to connect the multi-storey car park with Abington Street. The tram and the push cart have been replaced by a double-decker bus and a car. The double yellow lines also point to how busy this road becomes, especially on a Saturday afternoon.

NUNN MILLS

THE NAME NUNN Mills is a reference to the nuns of Delapré Abbey who once owned the site. The mill, pictured in around 1910, is a far later structure. It was owned by the firm of Westley Brothers and Clark. At this time milling was done by steam power and the grain transported by narrow boat. The firm later went on to become a limited company in 1919 before finally joining the Hovis Group in the 1940s. After a short spell of producing animal feeds, the site was acquired by Avon Cosmetics in 1968.

IN 2009 AVON opened their new European headquarters on the site. To the east of Avon Cosmetics is the derelict remains of Northampton Power Station, which was also known as Nunn Mills' Power Station. It was a source of power from the mid-1920s until its closure in 1975. Upon closing, the large concrete cooling towers were demolished. The main body of the building was retained and still stands today. Plans

have been submitted in the past for the redevelopment of the site but, as yet, the site is undeveloped. In graffiti circles Northampton Power Station is well known, perhaps even as far afield as Europe. The inward side of the building is decorated with an interesting array of street art. Northampton University currently plans to demolish the building and build a new £330 million waterside campus on the site. Construction could start in 2015, with the campus open by 2018. This is set within the framework of what is known as the South East Midlands Northampton Waterside Development Zone, as designated by the Coalition government in 2012. It will be just one of twenty sites along the river Nene which will be developed, hopefully creating an estimated 14,000 new jobs over a 120-hectare area.

For all of this change and development, the banks of the Nene are still enjoyed as a place of recreation, just as when the original photograph was taken. Young boys can still be seen playing and fishing along the banks.

BECKET'S WELL

THOMAS BECKET, AN Archbishop of Canterbury, was tried for treason at Northampton Castle in 1164. He was found guilty and imprisoned but subsequently escaped from St Andrew's Priory and made his way to France, where he stayed in exile until his return to England in 1170. Before beginning his long and arduous journey, Becket is said to have stopped at the well on Bedford Road to quench his thirst. As most people will know, Becket was martyred in Canterbury Cathedral on 29 December 1170, after his return to England. The Northampton Corporation decided to mark this event by rebuilding the well in a Gothic style. The well was moved from the centre of the carriageway and was rebuilt on the eastern side of the road. It was completed in 1843, as the stone carving on the front face, seen in this 1920 photograph, declares.

THE WELL-HOUSE was restored in 2006 by the Northampton Becket Rotary Club and Northampton Borough Council. A mosaic has been added to the interior of the well-house. The restoration also includes the addition of iron railings, which protect the interior from graffiti and other such anti-social activities. The rear view of the picture has been changed substantially by the ever-expanding hospital and more rapidly increasing heavy traffic on the Bedford Road. The wall which connected with the well-house has also been lowered. The increase in traffic has meant that the path which lined the other side of the road to Becket's Well has been removed and the entrance to Becket's Park is now further up the road near the junction with Victoria Promenade.

BECKET'S PARK

BECKET'S PARK, PHOTOGRAPHED in 1937. The park was known as Cow Meadow up until 1935. Its name was due to the fact that it was ' originally a piece of common land that was used by the townsfolk for the grazing of their animals. A common crime at the time was the illegal milking of cows on the meadow, once such a problem that a reward was offered to anyone who caught one of the criminal milkers. In 1703, a sum of £30 was made available for walks to be laid out and trees planted. These were extended in 1783 and later became known as Victoria Promenade. Between the parkland and Bedford Road was Becket's Walk. This was a tree-lined Victorian

promenade with strategically placed iron benches overlooking the park and the river Nene. In 1882 the Northampton Corporation took ownership of the land. The stone wall which lined the right-hand side of the park used to be capped with a cast-iron railing. There was also an entrance to the park opposite Becket's Well, which is now long gone.

THE PARK HAS always been on open land and has been extended and improved many times over the years. In the 1920s the bowling greens and the tennis courts were added, and in the 1930s boat rides began along the banks of the Nene. The most recent work to regenerate the area was the construction of an eighty-birth marina, which was completed in 2011. The park is still used for recreation and leisure today. It also hosts a variety of events each year, ranging from the Dragon Boat Race to welcoming the Olympic Torch relay in 2012.

DERNGATE

DERNGATE, SEEN HERE in around 1935, is one of the main entrance roads into Northampton's town centre. Its name derives from the Old English word *darn*, which means water. Therefore, the 'darn gate', as it was then known, simply meant the water gate, and was so named because it led down to the river Nene and the drinking wells. Although this is a very old street, the Great Fire of 1675 destroyed the original medieval buildings. The vast majority of the buildings now found on the street date from the nineteenth century, with a few notable examples from the twentieth. Two of the greatest architectural gems on the street are 78 Derngate and Bedford Mansions. Bedford Mansions comprises of a fine example of a 1930s Art Deco-style building. It was built to house luxury apartments in an era that believed the key to health and happiness was fresh, clean and simple housing combined with exposure to outdoor spaces. The flats fulfilled this remit, as they came with balconies and were within a short walking distance of Becket's Park and the river Nene. The most famous building on the street is 78 Derngate, one of the finest examples of Charles Rennie

Mackintosh's work. The building actually pre-dates Mackintosh, however, and goes back to approximately 1815. The building was built by William Mobbs, the great-grandfather of the First World War hero Edgar Mobbs. Mackintosh's involvement came much later, when the building was bought by Tom Lowke for his son, Wenman Bassett-Lowke, in 1917. Bassett-Lowke was interested in modern architecture and Mackintosh was recommended to him by a mutual friend. The work was carried out in 1917. It is not believed that Mackintosh visited the house during the reconstruction. However, he did visit in the early 1920s in connection with the redevelopment of the lounge and hall.

IN 1986 THE Derngate area was designated as a conservation area. The vast majority of its once-residential buildings are now used as business premises, though Bedford Mansions is still a residential block of flats. Number 78 Derngate, after many years of use by Northampton School for Girls, was listed in 1965 and was bought by the borough council in 1996. It is now a popular tourist attraction. The adjoining property is now a visitor and exhibition centre.

BILLING ROAD

BILLING ROAD, SEEN here in 1905, is just outside the boundary of the medieval town's walls. As a result, it is a relatively new development. The first development began when the new hospital was built, to the south of the road, in 1793. In 1845 the Northampton Corporation sold an area of land with the condition that only 'superior dwellings' should be built on it. A limited number were erected, but the rest of the area was left undeveloped until around the 1860s, when further 'superior' houses were erected. Rising numbers of middle-class professions were being drawn to these new suburban areas, and by 1882 around 20 per cent of the occupants of this new area were shoe manufacturers. The remainder was made up of other middle-class professions, including solicitors, bankers and clergymen. The shoe-manufacturer's workers only lived a stone's throw away, in rows of

terraced houses to the north of Billing Road. Although not as grand as the Victorian villas on Billing Road, they were far from slums and were of good construction.

ON 7 MARCH 2012 Billing Road was declared a conservation area by Northampton Borough Council due to its 'consistently high architectural style'. The large majority of the buildings in the road have not been substantially altered since the 1890s, though many are now business premises rather than family homes. This is not surprising when one considers how busy the road has become, and the lack of off-road parking provided by these Victorian properties. One area of the road, however, has suffered from the ravages of time: the cemetery. Built in 1847, it actually predates most of the Victorian villas. Today, it is overgrown and uncared for.

KING EDWARD VII MEMORIAL AND HOSPITAL

NORTHAMPTON'S FIRST HOSPITAL (pictured here in around 1900) opened in George Row on 29 March 1744. It was set up by philanthropic subscribers who hoped to provide the people of the county with a reliable source of treatment in an age where quacks were prevalent. It had the capacity to treat sixty inpatients at any one time, and in its first year treated a total of 182 patients. Its admission days were Wednesdays and Saturdays, with the exception of emergency cases. These days were chosen to coincide with local market days, allowing people to be brought in from the surrounding areas by cart; the carts would park up on Wood Hill. The popularity of the hospital increased until its location in George Row became unsuitable. In 1793 the new hospital opened up on the edge of town, at the corner of Billing Road. In 1835 the number of beds was increased in order to cope with a rise in the number of patients – many men were injured at this time

whilst building the London to Birmingham Express Railway. By the end of the century the hospital site had been expanded and a number of improvements had taken place, including the installation of electric lights in 1895. Between that date and the commencement of the National Health Service in 1948, Northampton Hospital continued to expand and improve – with the aid of generous local benefactors.

IN 1913 A MEMORIAL was added to the entrance to the hospital in order to commemorate the life of King Edward VII. It was paid for by public subscription and cost £1,200. Three days after its unveiling it was visited by King George V and Queen Mary. Today the hospital is an NHS Trust with room for up to 600 beds. It employs in excess of 4,000 staff over the 44-acre site. Its turnover now exceeds £190 million.

THE NEW THEATRE

ON THE LEFT-HAND side of Abington Street sits the New Theatre, which opened on
9 December 1912 (around the time when this photograph was taken). A range of shows were
on offer, including ballet, opera and musicals. Variety shows in particular, as at most theatres
of this era, were incredibly popular with working-class audiences. Up to 2,000 patrons could
be accommodated in the auditorium at one time. One noted visitor to the New Theatre was
Mr Winston Churchill. He did not see a show, but instead gave a political address in 1922.
However, the New Theatre started to go into decline after the Second World War when, like
many theatres all over the country, its audiences turned instead to cinema. With the advent
of television it became doubly difficult to compete. The line-up took a turn towards the
lowbrow in the final years of its life, with nude shows such as 'Strip! Strip! Hooray!' being

put on the bill. The New Theatre finally closed in 1958. It was demolished in 1960, and the site was then redeveloped and turned into a supermarket. It subsequently became a Primark store in the mid-1970s, as it remains to this day.

TODAY, THE VIEW has changed somewhat radically. Along with the New Theatre, many other old buildings in Abington Street were demolished to make way for post-war reconstruction. This, along with the arrival of the big chain stores, has turned one of Northampton's prime shopping streets into another generic high street, one that could be found anywhere in modern Britain. Although the general popularity of theatres has declined in the latter half of the twentieth century, Northampton can still boast a wide variety of cultural events and productions. The jewel in Northampton's crown, in terms of culture and the arts, is the Royal and Derngate. It has recently been subject to a £15 million redevelopment programme. The Royal and Derngate theatre offers a broad spectrum of productions – drama, dance, stand-up comedy and classical music – and a wide range of child-focused events. Over 350,000 people enjoy these productions every year.

THE CENTRAL LIBRARY

THE CENTRAL LIBRARY (seen here in 1910) is a very grand neo-classical-style building on Abington Street. It is the largest public library in Northamptonshire and is Grade II listed. It was built in 1910 and financed by the Scottish philanthropist Andrew Carnegie. Carnegie made his money in the American steel industry and was one of the greatest philanthropists of his age. He gave most of his money to causes that helped the working man, such as libraries.

TODAY THE CENTRAL LIBRARY is still in its original building but has benefited from various enlargements and improvements over the years. In order to try and keep up with modern society, the library is no longer solely a repository of books and articles: it now

offers toddler learning sessions, has a shop, loans DVDs and CDs, and conducts family activities. These improved and broadened services are brought together in the overarching title of Library Plus. Banners advertising Library Plus can now be seen outside of the library in order to encourage more townsfolk to use the facilities.

The two figures over the doors are John Dryden, the most famous poet and playwright of Restoration England, and Thomas Fuller, a prolific author of his age. Dryden and Fuller were both, curiously, born in Aldwincle, just north of Thrapston. The two figures in the centre are Andrew Carnegie and Lawrence Washington, who founded Northampton Grammar School. They were added a year after the library was completed in 1911.

FIRST WORLD WAR MEMORIAL

THE FIRST MEMORIAL to the dead of the First World War (seen here in 1919), before the erection of the permanent cenotaph in 1926, was in Abington Street. It was erected especially for Heroes Day, which was held on 7 September 1919. On that day over 8,000 local ex-servicemen marched past the memorial, replicating the event at the original cenotaph in Whitehall for the Victory Day Parade on 19 July. These parades marked the formal ending of the First World War and the signing of the Treaty of Versailles on 28 June 1919. Like most memorials of this period, it was made of wood and plaster. The stone memorials to the fallen that we know so well today came once the townspeople had raised enough money to commission a mason to create an eternal memorial.

THE CO-OPERATIVE BUILDING, seen in the earlier image behind the memorial, was replaced by a new Art Deco building in 1938, and is now subdivided by three modern high-street retailers. The entrance to H&M roughly marks the spot where the memorial once stood. Although the modern shop frontages have consumed the lower half of the building, the sweeping stylised lines of the Art Deco façade can be seen above. Today the memorial has long since gone: the permanent memorial is now located at the rear of All Saints' church.

ABINGTON STREET

THIS IMAGE SHOWS Abington Street
from another angle, *c.* 1936. Looking
to the east, the photograph shows the
Co-operative building, the Central Library
as well as the New Theatre. These buildings
were all built on the site of a series of
shops and houses, which were demolished
to make way for these grander buildings.
Before the Central Library was constructed
in 1910, a lane ran between these houses
which led to the old Tram Depot. This is
where the horse drawn trams and their
horses were kept.

ABINGTON STREET HAS become pedestrianised and is now Northampton's busiest shopping street. The old Co-operative building has been subdivided to comprise an H&M, a Poundland and a Sports Direct. The remodelled Art Deco frontage of the old Co-operative building can be seen in the modern image. The grandeur of the building with its clean and simple lines still remains, with only the lower part of the building remodelled to accommodate modern retailing.

In the distance, standing in the middle of what once was a public highway, is an art installation called Discovery. It celebrates the life and work of Francis Crick, who was born in Weston Favell in 1916. Professor Crick, along with his colleague James Watson, discovered the double helix structure in DNA. They later went on, along with Maurice Wilkins, to be awarded the Nobel Prize in 1962. The installation was erected in 2005.

MARKET SQUARE, EAST VIEW

NORTHAMPTON IS REPUTED to have the largest Market Square in England (pictured here in 1936). It was first given its market charter in 1189. The first market was held to the east side of All Saints' church but later moved, in 1235, to its current location when Henry III forbade the selling of goods in the churchyard. The market became the centre of the town when it was reconstructed after the Great Fire of 1675. The old fountain, which used to dominate the centre of the market, was erected in 1863 to mark the marriage of Prince Albert Edward, Prince of Wales, to Princess Alexandra of Denmark. The fountain was paid for by Captain Samuel Isaacs, a local shoe factory

magnate and commandant of the 5th Corps of the Northamptonshire Rifle Volunteers. The fountain was torn down by a team of workers over a two-day period in April 1962. It was removed when the Market Square was being regenerated and 'improved'.

ALTHOUGH THE LOCATION of the market has stayed the same since 1235, the surrounding buildings have been through many changes. The south and westerly sides of the market have survived well, but the north and easterly sides have suffered from a series of developments aimed at modernisation and reconstruction. The Grosvenor Centre, to the north of Market Square, is not the first shopping arcade to be located there. In 1972 the old Emporium Arcade was demolished to make way for the new shopping centre. The Emporium, built in 1901, fulfilled a similar place in society as its later replacement. It had a range of shops as well as a café, a hairdresser's and public conveniences. Peacock Place shopping centre now occupies the eastern side of the Market Square. It was once the location of the Peacock Hotel, a former coaching inn, and the offices of the *Northampton Herald* newspaper offices.

MARKET SQUARE,
WEST VIEW

IN 1911 A SERVICE of praise was held to mark the coronation of King George V. Two years later, in 1913, the King, along with Queen Mary, visited Northampton and gave a speech from a raised platform in Market Square. During the Second World War Market Square played host to Wings for Victory Week, Warship Week and Salute the Soldier Week. These events were all aimed at raising money for the war effort. The money raised during Warship Week paid for the construction of HMS *Laforey*. The surrender of Germany and

then Japan were both marked by large and joyous celebrations. After the war, Market Square played host to the Northamptonshire Regiment, who in June 1946 were given the Freedom of the Borough. This gave them the right to march through the town with bayonets fixed. This photograph of Market Square was taken in around 1910.

MARKETS ARE STILL held in Northampton today and run from Mondays to Saturdays. Monday's market is for fresh fruit and vegetables, cut flowers and plants. The rest of the week is devoted to a general market. In 2006 the Market Square was revamped and modernised. The market stalls were updated, changing from the old-fashioned tarpaulin structures to new rigid structures. An area was also created in order to allow space for events and entertainments, such as an ice-skating rink at Christmas. These improvements have only been met by partial success. The shopping centres and numerous out-of-town retail parks still retain a massive pull for townsfolk and visitors alike. Apart from numerous markets, there have been lots of other events of note that have taken place in Market Square over the years: celebrations, fairs – and even a riot. The riot took place in 1874 when supporters of Charles Bradlaugh protested at the outcome of a parliamentary by-election. They believed that the election result had been rigged. Both the police and the army were called. A personal appeal by Bradlaugh himself did nothing to stop the violence, and in the end rifles were fired to disperse the crowd.

MERCER'S ROW CORNER

HICKMANS MILLINERS IN 1914, which was once famed for its elaborate window displays. It stood on the corner of Mercer's Row and Market Square. On this site there once stood a series of public houses. The Queen's Dragoon was recorded as being there as early as 1676. This later changed its name to the Leg of Mutton and then, in 1814, it changed again to the Old Duke of Clarence. The building became unsafe and was demolished in 1911. The building which replaced it in 1912 then housed Hickmans and remains relatively unchanged till today.

During the Second World War, an ARP post was established in front of the building. This small sandbagged shelter was for the use of ARP Wardens during air raids. This was just opposite the old underground public toilets on Wood Hill, which were also used as an air-raid shelter.

HICKMANS IS NOW occupied by a Mace corner shop. The elaborate window displays and the ornate shop frontage have long since gone. These have been replaced by a generic modern shop frontage made of plastic and vinyl. Above Mace can be seen Faulkner's Barber Shop. Its

entrance is just visible to the left of the picture. The Mace store extends into the building next door, which can just be seen in the background. This modern angular building, which was built in the early 1960s to a design of A.W. Walker and Partners, was a replacement for Waterloo House, which once abutted Hickmans. Waterloo House is thought to have been constructed in around 1815, which would probably account for its name. The chimney stacks have vanished from the top of the building and have now been replaced by a small CCTV camera.

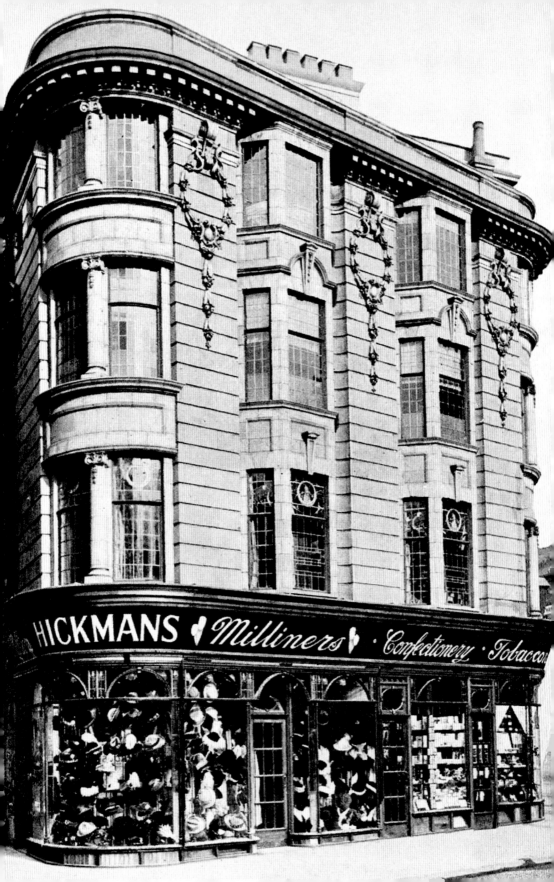

MERCER'S ROW

A MERCER IS a merchant or trader who deals specifically in textiles. Mercer's Row (pictured here in around 1915) got its name thanks to its close association with the textile trade. It adjoins the Drapery, which got its name in the fourteenth century in reference to the drapers who occupied the western side of the street. Although it is all known as the Drapery today, the eastern side of the street used to be known as 'the Glovery' because of the glovers who worked there. Running off Mercer's Row are two cut through lanes to Market Square, Conduit Lane and Drum Lane, both in use for hundreds of years. The combination of the narrow lane and the public houses lining either side of Drum Lane gives a hint of what the confined streets of medieval Northampton may have felt like. In 1745 a gate was erected at either end of Conduit Lane to prevent rubbish being deposited there – which proves that littering is not a totally modern phenomenon.

APART FROM THE modern alterations to the shop frontages, the overall architectural nature of Mercer's Row remains the same. The independent businesses which once filled the row, such as the Geisha Restaurant and Café, have been replaced by household names like Toni & Guy and Greggs, the bakers. The Westminster Bank, which was built in 1925 on the corner of Mercer's Row and the Drapery, has now been turned into a branch of the Nationwide building society.

ELECTRIFIED TRAMS

NORTHAMPTON'S ORIGINAL TRAM network was established in 1881 by the
Northampton Street Tramway Company. Unlike in this picture from 1932, all of the
trams of that period were horse-drawn. The original network lasted less than thirteen
years, ending when the Northampton Corporation purchased the company for £38,700.
New track was laid and an electrified system was up and running by 1904. The mayor
inaugurated the new tram network on 21 July. Over 42,000 people used the new trams

on the first weekend alone. This shows how much of a novelty this new mode of transport was in Edwardian Northampton. There were thirty-seven trams in Northampton's tram fleet. The clearly visible number ten on the tram tells us that this is one of the original twenty trams which came into service in 1904. The livery of the trams was a very smart vermilion and white. The tram network finally closed in December 1934. The last tram departed Mercer's Row, filled with civic representatives of the town, and made its way back to the depot in St James' Road for the last time.

ALTHOUGH THE TRAM has started to make a comeback in larger cities such as Manchester and Nottingham, the mainstay of public transport in Northampton is now the bus. It was the rise of the motor bus which ultimately saw the demise of the tram. Trams could never match the flexibility of the bus, as additional bus routes could be added to the ever-expanding Northampton in the 1930s without the need to disrupt traffic with the laying of new track. To add insult to injury, the buses also took over the tram depot on St James' Road. Mercer's Row is now home to Northampton's central taxi rank. An elongated line of taxis, waiting for fares, can be seen here both day and night.

THE CENOTAPH AND WOOD HILL

THE CENOTAPH WAS erected on the east side of All Saints' churchyard in honour and in memory of those who fell in the First World War. It was unveiled by General Lord Horne on 11 November 1926 (around about the time when this photograph was taken). It was designed by the renowned architect Sir Edwin Lutyens, who was also responsible for the design of the national cenotaph in Whitehall, London. On 7 July the next year the Prince of Wales visited Northampton and laid a wreath at the cenotaph. It was later updated to record the names of those who fell during the Second World War. Wood Hill got its name

from the wood market which once took place there on Wednesdays and Saturdays. The edifice was later used as a dispersal point for the carrier carts which would transport people and goods to and from the surrounding villages to the market. These carts were used to bring the sick to the hospital on the adjoining George Row. It later became a taxi rank for the new motor taxis and buses. Today the taxi rank has been moved around the corner to Mercer's Row. The cenotaph on Wood Hill is still the focus for the town's annual Remembrance Service on 11 November. However, today the townspeople remember those who have been lost in all of Britain's wars along with the fallen of the First World War.

THE CONTEMPORARY PHOTOGRAPH shows a couple of the town's younger generation enjoying a carefree Saturday morning riding their bicycles in Wood Hill. They make for a stark contrast against the memorial to the young men who had such pleasures stolen from them. To the right of the youths there used to be a kiosk, paid for by public subscription, to benefit a local ex-serviceman who had lost his limbs in the First World War. It was known as Eckford's Kiosk.

THE GUILDHALL

IN THE VICTORIAN era a Town Hall was the literal embodiment of a town and the ornate embellishments were a product of the desire to impress visitors. It was very much a way for a town to show off its wealth and prosperity. Northampton's Guildhall, seen here in 1922, stands a testament to the prosperity of the town in that era, primarily attained through its involvement in the boot and shoe industry. Northampton's old Town Hall stood at the corner of Abington Street and Wood Hill. It was sold by auction on 25 July 1864 and fetched £1,200. The sale of the old Town Hall represented the growing trend for modernisation and improvement in Victorian Northampton. The new Guildhall, sited in St Giles' Square, opened on 17 May 1864 after three years of construction work. It was opened by the mayor, Councillor Mark Dorman. In celebration, a public holiday was declared. The building was designed by Edward William Godwin in the neo-Gothic style. It was embellished by ornate carvings and inlayed with decorative stone. The original design was symmetrical. This symmetry was lost in 1892 when the Guildhall was extended westward towards Wood Hill.

IN 1992 ANOTHER extension was undertaken to the east of the existing Guildhall. The modern extension was far less architecturally sympathetic to the original structure than the 1892 extension. Today the Guildhall not only houses Northampton Borough Council but also the record of births, marriages and deaths as well as a registry office and conference space. In 2002 a memorial to Diana, Princess of Wales was added. It was unveiled by her brother, the 9th Earl Spencer, in the presence of Michael Geoffrey Boss, the mayor of Northampton.

GEORGE ROW

THE SESSIONS HOUSE can be seen here on the right-hand side of the picture, *c.* 1910. It was probably the first building to be completed after the Great Fire of 1675. It was built in a baroque style and completed in 1678. The Sessions House was used for a variety of legal sessions, including the Quarter Sessions and the Assize Courts. Quarter Sessions were held four times a year and dealt with both criminal and administrative matters. Criminal sessions were held by a justice of the peace. For more serious matters, judges would come up from London, twice a year, to hold the Assize Courts. These were terminated in 1972 when permanent Crown Courts were established. In the eighteenth century these criminal cases were treated as great sources of entertainment by townsfolk. The crowds surrounding the courts for notorious cases were often large, and many a judge found it difficult to control them.

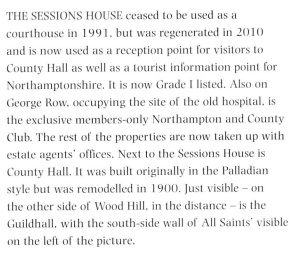

THE SESSIONS HOUSE ceased to be used as a courthouse in 1991, but was regenerated in 2010 and is now used as a reception point for visitors to County Hall as well as a tourist information point for Northamptonshire. It is now Grade I listed. Also on George Row, occupying the site of the old hospital, is the exclusive members-only Northampton and County Club. The rest of the properties are now taken up with estate agents' offices. Next to the Sessions House is County Hall. It was built originally in the Palladian style but was remodelled in 1900. Just visible – on the other side of Wood Hill, in the distance – is the Guildhall, with the south-side wall of All Saints' visible on the left of the picture.

GEORGE HOTEL

THE GEORGE HOTEL (seen here in 1905) used to be one of the grandest and most important buildings in Northampton. In earlier times it was a fine coaching inn providing a resting place for travellers on the road to London. The earliest known inn on this site is recorded as 1555. The original George was burnt down during the Great Fire and was rebuilt again on nearly the same site as the original. The new George was set back from the original building, allowing the road to be widened to allow for the increase in traffic. The building was subsequently modernised in the nineteenth century. In the seventeenth and eighteenth centuries it was a key building in the town, providing a venue for a variety of social

and public activities. It was used for balls, dinners and concerts, as well as public meetings and lectures. The building's importance in town life declined as new public buildings took over as official meeting places. Trade for the George also started to decline as the railways took over from the coaching routes. One of the George's claims to fame is that, in 1844, Queen Victoria, whilst on her way to the Burghley estate, once gave a speech outside of the building from her carriage.

BY THE EARLY years of the twentieth century the George had gone into decline. It lost its license in 1916 and the owners eventually sold the building for £20,000. It was demolished in 1921. The building was replaced by a Lloyds Bank. Today the building is still used by Lloyds, though now in the guise of Lloyds TSB. Its cash machine is a now a key stopping point for late-night revellers on their way to enjoy the various bars which now line either side of Bridge Street.

ALL SAINTS' CHURCH

TO THIS DAY, on 29 May each year, Oak Apple Day is celebrated at All Saints' church (pictured here in around 1900). The tradition demands that an oak leaf garland is placed around the statue of King Charles II which stands on the portico overlooking the Drapery. This is done to recognise the gift of 100 tons of timber from the royal forest at Salcey which he donated after the Great Fire. He also waived the chimney tax in order to help the townsfolk pay for the reconstruction work. There had been a church on the

site since Norman times, but the church in 1675 was a medieval construction. Much of the medieval church was destroyed by the fire, but the tower and the crypt survived. The church was rebuilt in stone in the classical style, though the medieval tower was retained. In addition, a courtyard was created in the front of the portico which was enclosed by iron railings. These, unfortunately, have not survived.

TODAY THE CHURCH is still an active place of worship with both a boys' and a girls' choir. It also has a company of bell ringers. A recent addition in 2008 saw the development of the vestry into a commercially-leased coffee shop called the John Clare Lounge. It also has seating outside, underneath the portico. Although a slightly unusual arrangement for a church, the coffee shop does encourage those of a non-religious persuasion to enter the church and enjoy its architectural splendour. A more spiritual addition was added in the 1920s in the form of a ladies' or memorial chapel. It was dedicated to those who lost their lives in the First World War.

THE DRAPERY

THE DRAPERY, 1950. On the right-hand side of the picture are two buildings which would have been familiar to most of the townsfolk doing their shopping on a Saturday afternoon in the 1950s: the National Provincial and Adnitt's. The grand neo-classical building of the National Provincial Bank was an amalgamation of the Northamptonshire Union Bank, which was based at the bank from 1836, and the National Provincial and Union Bank of England. Originally the building was called Percival's Bank. Through an amalgamation of its own, it then became the Northamptonshire Union Bank. The phoenix which can be seen at the top of the building was used on all of their cheques and banknotes. In January 1970 the bank became a National Westminster. The NatWest, as it is known today, is still operating from this location. Next door to the bank is the

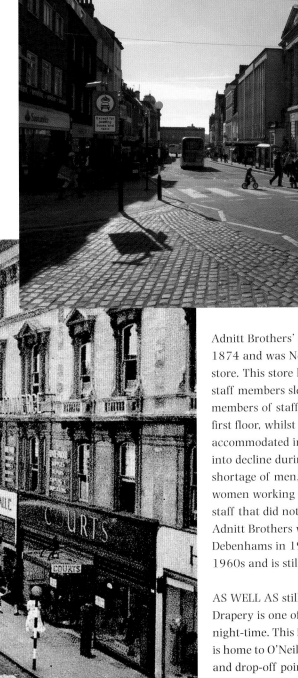

Adnitt Brothers' department store. It opened in 1874 and was Northampton's first department store. This store had an unusual practice: all of its staff members slept on the premises; the female members of staff were accommodated on the first floor, whilst the male members of staff were accommodated in Swan Yard. This practice went into decline during the First World War as the shortage of men, and the increased number of women working in industry, meant that hiring staff that did not 'live in' became necessary. The Adnitt Brothers were eventually bought out by Debenhams in 1952. The shop was rebuilt in the 1960s and is still trading today.

AS WELL AS still being a busy shopping street, the Drapery is one of Northampton's busiest streets at night-time. This is due to a few key factors. Firstly, it is home to O'Neill's bar. Secondly, it is a busy pickup and drop-off point for taxis. Thirdly, and most importantly, it is home to a late-night McDonald's restaurant, which does become very popular, in the early hours of the morning, with revellers.

BRIDGE STREET

THE BAY WINDOW which can be seen halfway up the street on the eastern side of the 1906 image belongs to the Angel Hotel. As a coaching inn, it served the town's main road to and from London. It was one of the main post houses in Northampton and dates back to the sixteenth century. At the bottom of Bridge Street are the remains of the Chapel of St John, founded in 1138. It provided food and shelter for both the poor and for travellers. It also contained an infirmary, which later became an almshouse. After the Battle of Northampton, during the War of the Roses, many soldiers were treated at the chapel. Those that did not survive were buried in the grounds. Much of the building that we can

see today is of the fifteenth and sixteenth century. When the John Street railway station was opened in 1872, the chapel was used as a storage space; then, in 1877, it was sold and made into a Catholic church.

IN 2005 THE chapel was redeveloped and turned into a high-end restaurant called the Church Bar and Restaurant. The railway station, along with some of the historic buildings to the south of Bridge Street, was demolished in 1960 to make way for office blocks and a multi-storey car park. Today the old Angel Hotel is better known as the Fat Cat Café and Bar. This popular nightspot was hit by fire on 2 January 2012. The fire was so intense that it took fifty fire-fighters to extinguish the blaze. The inside of this historic building was gutted, and it is currently surrounded by building supports and scaffolding.

BOOTS

BOOTS, *c.* 1950. This building
stands on the corner of the Drapery
and Gold Street. The photograph
was captured before the islands
were removed to improve the flow
of the traffic. Before the shopping
centres were constructed, Boots was
centrally located at the crossroads of
Northampton's busiest retail streets.
On 14 July 1941, Boots, along with
many other historic buildings on Gold
Street and George Row, miraculously
avoided destruction when a Stirling
Bomber crashed in the town
centre. The Stirling was from No. 7
Squadron, based at RAF Oakingham.
It was trying to return to base after
receiving heavy flak damage over the
Continent. The aircraft came down in
Gold Street, with the wings scoring

the buildings either side of the street. The fuselage, still armed with bombs, continued on to George Row, where it exploded into flames. The crew had steered the aircraft clear of the town, but unfortunately it went on to circle and come around again. The only fatality was the pilot, Flight Sergeant Madgwick, who fell out of his parachute whilst descending to earth. T.C. Palmer's, opposite Boots, received particularly bad damage due to its numerous glazed window panels.

T.C. PALMER'S AND Boots have long since moved, to be replaced by other modern retailers, but the splendour of the buildings still lives on. H. Samuel, on the other hand, which was located on the Drapery next to Boots, is still present today, although it has moved one door along to a post-war building of less architectural merit than its original location.

GOLD STREET

GOLD STREET, *c.* 1934. This is one of
Northampton's oldest streets. During Roman
times it was the main road from Duston to
Irchester. The street once stood within the walls
of the original Saxon defences (which would
later become Northampton Castle). In the
twelfth century the street was one of the first to
be paved. The name Gold Street is a reference
to the fact that it was, along with nearby
Silver Street, the centre for money exchange in
Northampton. It was, at the time, renowned for
its large Jewish population. By the nineteenth
century Gold Street was one of the busiest
shopping streets in the town. It boasted such
household names as Lipton's Tea and, by 1915,
a Woolworth's store.

TODAY GOLD STREET is no longer the heart of Northampton's retail district. The arrival of large indoor shopping centres during the 1970s has meant that the higher-class shops have been drawn to the eastern side of town. Gold Street is now home to a combination of 'bargain' stores and charity shops. After years of neglect and decay, Gold Street has recently experienced a facelift. Over £6 million has been spent on improving the pavement and street furniture all the way from Marefair through to Gold Street. This coincided with the redevelopment of the Grand Hotel and Old Dolphin Bar. This magnificently grand Victorian building was closed for many years and declined into a state of considerable disrepair. In 2010 it was reopened as a Travelodge. What was then a fifty-seven-room hotel was transformed, both internally and externally, and the hotel now has sixty-five bedrooms. In total, £2.3 million was spent on the redevelopment of the building.

GOLD STREET AND MAREFAIR

ON THE CORNER of Gold Street and Horseshoe Street, seen here in around 1900, is the site of the town's first tavern and music hall, which opened in 1855. It was also here, in the early twentieth century, that both Charlie Chaplin and Gracie Fields performed before they reached 'the big time'. The Palace of Varieties occupied the site from 1901 until 1912, when it was turned into the Picture House. In 1913 it was taken over by a Mr Leon Vint, who opened it as Vint's Palace, a music hall which showed pictures. By 1919 it had

been transformed again, to become The Majestic. The Majestic closed down in 1937 and the building stood empty. After many different owners and name changes, the building was demolished in 1950 and a shop was opened on the site in 1952.

THE BUILDING IS now occupied by a mobile phone shop and repair centre. A recent development in this area of town was the opening of Sol Central in 2002 on the opposite side of the road to the former home of Vint's Palace. It is an entertainment centre that includes a Vue cinema which boasts ten screens and can sit 2,547 people at once – a number which surely would have impressed Mr Vint if he had been alive today, especially if he knew how much a modern-day cinema ticket costs.

HAZELRIGG HOUSE

OFTEN KNOWN AS Cromwell House, Hazelrigg House (seen here in around 1910) sits in Marefair and is one of the oldest buildings in town. It dates back to the sixteenth century and is built in the Tudor style. It is supposed to have got its name from a family who once owned the house. In its day, it would have been a very grand building. It was one of the few buildings in Northampton to have survived the Great Fire of 1675, most probably because it was constructed of stone – its lost contemporaries would have been constructed mainly of wood and thatch. The association with Oliver Cromwell came at a later date. Local legend tells us that Cromwell stayed in the house before defeating Charles I's army at the Battle of Naseby in 1645. It must be pointed out, however, that various other buildings in the county also make this claim. Either he couldn't find a comfortable room, or some of these tales have been made up over the years.

AS TASTES CHANGED, and newer and grander houses were constructed in the Victorian era, Hazelrigg House went into decline. It was reduced in size and was split up into three separate dwellings. In the twentieth century the house was used by a variety of different occupants as an office and meeting space. By the 1980s it had become dilapidated. It was saved from further decay in 1988 when it was conserved as part of the surrounding development of flats and offices. It is now owned by Northampton Borough Council and is used as a children's nursery. Apart from child-friendly window paintings, the house is in good order and has been kept true to its original design. The grandiose stature that Hazelrigg House once enjoyed is today somewhat overshadowed by the enormity that is Sol Central's entertainment centre nearby.

THE RACECOURSE

BEFORE COMING TO an end in 1904, race meetings were held at Northampton's racecourse for over 180 years (seen here in around 1935). The Jockey Club finally banned the meetings due to a series of accidents between the years of 1901 and 1904. The problem with the 118-acre site was its rights of way: there were various rights of way across the course that could not be fenced off. Without these safety improvements, the racecourse could not be brought up to scratch and therefore the site could no longer function as a racecourse. The course was also deemed to be too short. Thereafter, the racecourse was used solely as a recreational space, the exception being during both the First and the Second World Wars, when the site was used by the military as an encampment. The wooden huts and barracks which occupied the site were not completely demolished until 1953.

TODAY THE RACECOURSE is used as a park and recreation area. In recent years a lot of money has been spent on improving the course's facilities. These include new changing rooms for the many Sunday League football teams which use the park's eighteen football pitches, and a children's adventure playground. There is also a rugby pitch, seven cricket pitches, six tennis courts and three bowling greens. The grandstand, which is no longer quite so grand these days, is now used as a Chinese restaurant. One of the most well-known events to be held at the racecourse in recent times was the Northampton Balloon Festival. It was held on the site from 1990 to 2008. This popular event moved from the racecourse when the borough council decided that, due to budget cuts, they could no longer afford to host the event. Since 2009 the Balloon Festival has been held at Billing Aquadrome.

THE WHITE ELEPHANT

TOWARDS THE END of the nineteenth century this part of Northampton was an up and coming area with many large town houses being constructed overlooking the racecourse. As part of that growth, The White Elephant was built in 1883. It stood on the corner of St Matthew's Parade and Kingsley Road and was originally called the Kingsley Park Hotel. It was built by a syndicate of sporting gentleman who wished to capitalise upon the visitors to the nearby racecourse. Unfortunately, the racecourse closed in 1904 and their source of business dried up. The name was changed to The White Elephant, for obvious reasons, in the 1950s when it was opened as a public house.

In the picture, from around 1906, you can see the No. 11 tram making its way towards St James. The trams stopped just the other side of the road to the Kinglesy Park Hotel. The original tram stop is still there and is one of only two left in Northampton. The other one,

in Kingsthorpe, is in a far greater state of repair and is not covered in graffiti as this example is.

TO MANY TOWNSFOLK, The White Elephant is something of a local landmark. The White Elephant sign is not the original but a replacement. The whereabouts of the original sign is unknown. The pub did undergo a brief name change in recent years but popular demand resulted in the original name being reinstated. Apart from the Kingsley Park Garage and the alterations to the road junction, the view is reasonably unchanged. Today this road junction is particularly busy. A long period of time was spent waiting for an interval in the traffic in which to take this photograph!

DALLINGTON

DALLINGTON WAS ONCE a village on the outskirts of Northampton. This photograph of Dallington was taken in around 1930. It was mentioned in the Domesday Book and was originally recorded as Dailintone. Like many other villages that once surrounded Northampton, Dallington is no longer a separate entity. It was absorbed in 1932 when the town was expanding its suburban housing estates, and was completely surrounded in the 1950s by the Kings Heath housing estate. Although surrounded by a council-built estate, it does still retain some of the character of an English country village. It is quiet, sedate and a desirable place to live. Luckily, it was designated a conservation area of 'distinctive character worthy of preservation' in January 1970. The Spencer family of Althorp have had a long connection with Dallington, most recently when the manor returned to the family in 1867. They owned the manor until the early twentieth century, when they sold

their land to the Northampton Corporation in order to facilitate their suburban expansion plans. The Spencer family retain their historical ties and still play an important role as patrons of the village.

THE CURRENT EARL Spencer is still required to choose the parish priest in consultation with the Bishop of Peterborough and representatives from the parish council. Pictured here, we see the village green and an old row of cottages that line the stream. One of the cottages used to be the village blacksmith's, but it is now a residential property. Due to the conservation area designation, thankfully, not much has changed from this vantage point. Dallington still has a church, a hall, a beautiful village green and an eighteenth-century thatched public house, The Wheatsheaf. It is one of only thirteen buildings in the whole borough that is thatched. It still maintains some open space in the form of Dallington Park, which was originally part of the grounds of the manor house. When the land was given to the council it came with the condition that it never be used for development.

DALLINGTON
ALMSHOUSES

THESE BEAUTIFUL SANDSTONE almshouses (seen
here in around 1920) were given to the village in
1673 by Sir Richard Raynsford. Raynsford was a
lawyer, judge and MP for Northampton; he later
went on to become chief justice of the King's
Bench under King Charles II. He lived in Dallington
Manor, and on his death, in 1680, he was buried in
St Mary's churchyard. The almshouses were built
with the purpose of housing two old men and two
old women, all paupers, who had lived and worked
in the village. The building, in its original form,
would most probably have had a thatched roof. The
Latin inscription on the face of building reads, 'Let
none dare to violate them, vengeance is God's.' He
also established an almshouse at Chapel Brampton.

THANKFULLY, THIS IS one of the few images of Northampton that has remained unchanged over time. Apart from the oak tree on the green maturing, little discernible change has occurred since the original picture was taken. The oak tree is now 102 years old. It was planted on 22 June 1911 in order to commemorate the coronation of King George V. Today the almshouses are still in use as charitable housing for the needy. They are currently being managed by Northampton Borough Council and assigned trustees. The Grade II listed building was restored in 1957. It has recently benefited from another restoration, and is in fine condition. The grounds are well kept in the finest traditions of English cottage gardens. The stone wall, which surrounds the building, is not original and was added sometime after the 1890s. Next door, of similar ironstone construction, is the village hall, which was erected far later in 1840 and was originally used as the village school. In the distance is what is now known as Raynsford Road.

ST JAMES' END AND CAFÉ SQUARE

THE NAME 'ST JAMES' derives from the Augustinian Abbey of St James, which was founded in around 1104 and was dissolved in 1538. It was sited at what is now the Express Lifts' site. An archaeological dig in 2000, carried out before the construction of a new housing development, found the remains of the abbey. In addition to the abbey, the graves of 300 people were found in its cemetery. This picture, taken in 1906, shows the part of St James' End known as Café Square. The square was known by this name for many years because of the presence of the well-known

and much-loved Althorp Café, which is centrally placed in the picture. It later went on to be converted into a local bank and is today a NatWest. When this photograph was taken, the café was at the corner of a crossroads which connected Althorp Road with St James' Road. The road has since been closed, however, and it is no longer a crossroads. The church tower, which cannot be seen in the old photograph, was added to St James's church after the First World War in remembrance of those men of the parish who did not return home.

FURTHER ALONG ST JAMES' Road, heading towards the town centre on the right-hand side, is Church's Shoe Factory. It was established in 1873 by Thomas Church. Church's, unlike many other shoe manufacturers in Northamptonshire, has managed to stay in business. At the height of the shoe trade in the 1940s, when Northampton was producing boots for both the domestic market as well as the British Army, there were 240 shoe manufacturers in the county. Today there are only thirty-four. It is perhaps Church's reputation for quality that has ensured its survival. Until recently, the Prada fashion group had a majority share in the business.

ST JAMES' END
TO WEEDON ROAD

ANOTHER VIEW OF St James' End, this time looking away from the town centre towards Weedon Road in 1907. To the right-hand side of the image can be seen the Althorp Café. The photographer seems to have drawn a crowd of school children, all complete with their school caps, making way for the No. 15 tram for Kingsley Park.

A little bit further up on Weedon Road is Franklin's Gardens. It was originally known as Melbourne Gardens until 1886 when a local hotelier, John Franklin, purchased the site and renamed it after himself. It was originally a park with an ornamental garden, cricket pitch and an ornamental lake. The Saints' Rugby Football team didn't move in

until the late 1880s. Their ground slowly started to improve after the Second World War and today Franklin's Gardens is a modern stadium with a capacity of 13,500 (with an additional forty-eight executive boxes). They currently have plans to increase their capacity to 15,500.

THE BUILDINGS IN the centre of the picture are now a branch of Nationwide and on the right a branch of Lloyds TSB. The road network has also changed. As can be seen from the modern image, it is now a main road into Northampton. The Weedon Road links directly with the M1, which accounts for the extremely busy nature of the road.

On the left-hand side of the picture a modern row of shops, which service the three blocks of flats, can just be seen. This post-war development now dominates this end of St James. The buildings in the original photograph, including the tavern, have all been demolished.

KINGSTHORPE AND THE COCK INN

KINGSTHORPE WAS ONCE a village on the outskirts of Northampton. In 1900 the majority of the village became a part of Northampton, whilst the remaining outlying areas became a part of Boughton and Moulton. By 1931 these areas had also been absorbed by the ever-expanding borough. The Cock Inn stands on the old village green, as seen in this photograph from 1899. This is the only part of Kingsthorpe which still bears any resemblance to its former life as a village. The present Cock Inn only dates back to 1893, when it replaced another coaching inn of the same name. The trams used to run down the

centre of Harborough Road and, until they were replaced by buses in 1934, went to the centre of town. Also visible on the green is a war memorial and a fountain which marks Queen Victoria's Diamond Jubilee in 1897.

BOTH PHOTOGRAPHS WERE taken at the corner of Mill Lane by the outward boundary of Thornton's Park. This is the rough location of the old toll house, which once served this stretch of road. Also near this location was the King's Well. Local legend says that it was purer than the town's piped water supply, and that in all of its history it had never once frozen. Visible on the green is one of the old tram stops. The buildings past the green are now gone and have been replaced by the grounds of the Good Shepherd Catholic Primary School.

THORNTON'S PARK

THORNTON'S PARK, ALSO known as Kingsthorpe Park, *c.* 1950. It was once the garden
to Thornton's Hall. Designed by a Mr John Johnson of Leicester, the hall is a fantastic
example of Georgian architecture. One of its prime features was its particularly fine spiral
staircase with wrought-iron balustrades, lit by a lantern dome. The hall dates back to
approximately 1775 and was used as a home by a succession of families. It was acquired
by the Northampton Corporation in 1938. The hall and park was purchased from the
Thornton family, who had inherited the house. In 1939 the parkland was opened to
the public for recreation and leisure. The parkland consisted of 15 acres of lawns and
ornamental gardens. It was well known locally for its large and colourful flower beds. The
large wall, which once enclosed the hall, was reduced in height in 1965 to open the space

up and improve the site's appearance. Unfortunately, the ornamental pond was filled in by the council in the 1970s. The cedar trees, which are as much of a local landmark as the hall, still remain today and are believed to be as old as the hall itself.

TODAY BOTH THE hall and parkland are in a sorrowful state of repair. Community groups used the hall until recently, when high levels of radon gas were detected. It has also been subjected to a series of arson attacks, leaving it in a poor state of repair. Currently the hall, which is Grade II listed, is in the hands of a private developer. The ornamental walls and pathways are crumbling and are in desperate need of repair. The floral beds, once a prime feature of the park, are long gone. There is, perhaps, now hope for Thornton's Park, however, as a local community group has been formed with the aim of reclaiming what was once a beautiful local resource.

ELEANOR CROSS

THE ELEANOR CROSS, seen here in 1922, was erected in 1294. It was erected by King Edward I in order to commemorate the stopping place of his wife's funeral cortège. It took three years for the cross to be completed, with work starting in 1291. Queen Eleanor's funeral cortège processed from Lincoln, where her body was embalmed, to London and her final resting place at Westminster Abbey. The funeral cortège stopped at Delapré Abbey on 9 December 1290. The journey took fifteen days to complete. It stopped at fifteen separate locations along the 159-mile route. King Edward requested that his master mason, Richard Crundale, design a cross which could be erected at the stopping places of the funeral cortège. Crosses were erected at twelve of the fifteen stopping places. Of the twelve crosses erected, only three

are still standing today. Two of these crosses are in Northamptonshire. The second cross is at Geddington, near Kettering.

NORTHAMPTON'S CROSS IS in a good state of repair, when its age is taken into account, but it is missing its crowning column and finial. The date when the cross was damaged is unknown. The monument has been repaired many times over the years. The biggest repair took place in 1884, when the stone steps at the base were replaced. They were weather-worn due to being made of local sandstone. There have also been various smaller repairs over the years. As well as the marks of the stonemasons who have repaired it over the years, it also bears many marks of graffiti. Graffiti is not a modern phenomenon, as the ancient names and initials carved on the cross clearly prove. The busy A508 now runs alongside this cross. It is one of the main links from central Northampton to the A45. The serenity which the cross once enjoyed, in the shadow of Delapré Abbey, has been removed forever by twentieth-century townsfolk's reliance upon the car.

If you enjoyed this book, you may also be interested in…

Northamptonshire: A Portrait in Pen & Ink
CLIVE HOLMES

Collated from the series 'Around the County' in the *Northamptonshire Chronicle & Echo*, this book contains over ninety of Clive Holmes' popular images of the area. Focusing on a variety of subjects, from rivers and cottages to churches and manor houses, the outstanding architectural heritage and natural beauty of Northamptonshire is portrayed in a unique and fascinating style.

978 0 7524 5351 4

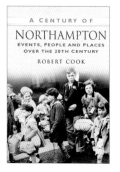

A Century of Northampton
ROBERT COOK

Here is a selection of photographs which illustrate the transformation that has taken place in Northampton during the twentieth century. This book offers an insight into the daily lives and living conditions of local people and gives the reader glimpses and details of familiar places during a century of unprecedented change.

978 0 7509 4929 3

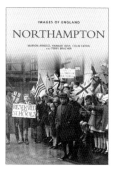

Northampton
MARIAN ARNOLD, HANNAH JOSH, COLIN EATON AND TERRY BRACHER

A collection of more than 180 old photographs that traces some of the many ways in which Northampton has changed and developed, and the ways in which it has remained untouched. This work records various aspects of everyday life, from shops and businesses, churches and schools, to images of work and leisure, day trips and days off.

978 0 7524 3836 8

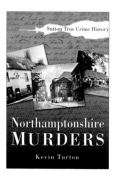

Northamptonshire Murders
KEVIN TURTON

An exploration of murders in Northamptonshire from 1852 to 1952. A chapter is devoted to each murder featured. Kevin Turton covers not only the events and subsequent investigation but also the trial of the killer and public reaction to the crime. Featuring many illustrations, including newspaper cuttings, penny dreadfuls, and photographs of the crime scenes as they are today, this book is a comprehensive reference to the county's dark past.

978 0 7509 3329 2

Visit our website and discover thousands of other History Press books.
www.thehistorypress.co.uk